D1532647

A Kid's Guide to
MYTHOLOGY

JASON

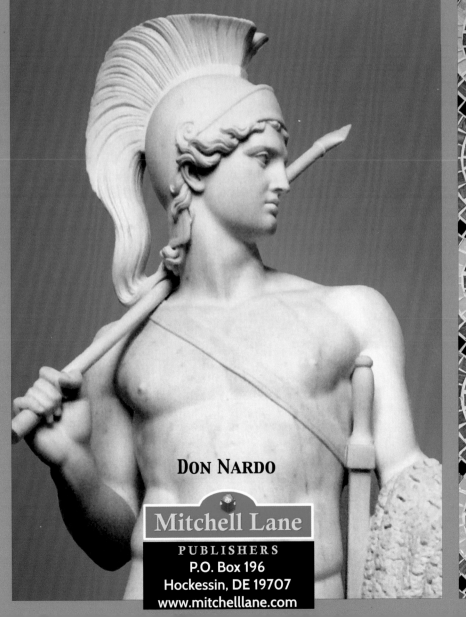

DON NARDO

Mitchell Lane
PUBLISHERS
P.O. Box 196
Hockessin, DE 19707
www.mitchelllane.com

Mitchell Lane

PUBLISHERS

Printing   1   2   3   4   5   6   7   8

Apollo
Athena
Hercules
Jason

Odysseus
Poseidon
Thor
Zeus

Library of Congress Cataloging-in-Publication Data
Nardo, Don, 1947- author.
Jason / by Don Nardo.
     pages cm. — (A kid's guide to mythology)
 Audience: 8-11.
 Audience: Grades 3-6.
 Includes bibliographical references and index.
 ISBN 978-1-68020-008-9 (library bound)
 1. Jason (Greek mythology)—Juvenile literature. 2. Argonauts (Greek mythology)—Juvenile literature. 3. Mythology, Greek—Juvenile literature. 4. Mythology in literature—Juvenile literature. I. Title.
 BL820.A8N37 2016
 398.20938'02—dc23
                                                                                    2015005446

eBook ISBN: 978-1-61228-009-6

PUBLISHER'S NOTE: The Internet sites referenced herein were active as of the publication date. Due to the fleeting nature of some web sites, we cannot guarantee they will all be active when you are reading this book.

To reflect current usage, we have chosen to use the secular era designations BCE ("before the common era") and CE ("of the common era") instead of the traditional designations BC ("before Christ") and AD (anno Domini, "in the year of the Lord").

DISCLAIMER: Many versions of each myth exist today. The author is covering only one version of each story. Other versions may differ in details.

CONTENTS

Words in **bold** throughout can be found in the Glossary.

Found in a house in the ancient Roman city of Pompeii, this painting shows the infamous one-sandaled man— the Greek hero Jason.

A Hero for the Ages

In the fabulous annals of ancient Greek mythology, few characters are as famous as Jason (JAY-sin). He appears in several myths. His most renowned deed was finding the Golden Fleece. That gleaming hide of a special, magical ram had long rested in Colchis (KOLE-chuss), a remote land located on the Black Sea's eastern coast. Jason and the men who accompanied him on his quest became known as the Argonauts. This was because their ship was the *Argo*, named after Argus (AHR-gis), the man who built the vessel.

To the ancient Greeks, Jason's epic voyage to find the Fleece was a heroic act of the highest order. So he joined the ranks of the heroes, a small number of unusually brave and daring men who are especially celebrated in the Greek myths. They were larger-than-life individuals who took on tasks that most other people lacked the courage and skill to face. Heroes' deeds "often had vital effects on human lives," modern myth-teller Philip Wilkinson writes. They "founded tribes and cities, killed monsters, and provided the necessities of life."[1]

Myth, Magic, and Adventure

Another common element found in the myths of the Greek heroes is their frequent interaction with the gods. Jason was no exception. He and the other Argonauts encountered several of those divine beings during their travels. The ancient Greeks believed that nature and humanity were governed by a great many gods. Each one, the Greeks thought, commanded certain aspects of life and the world. For example, powerful Poseidon (poh-SY-din) ruled the seas. And swift-footed Hermes (HER-meez) was both the messenger of the gods and the protector of travelers. In that latter capacity, he often visited Jason and his comrades during their journey.

The Greeks believed that the deities had personalities very much like those of humans. "They loved and hated and quarreled with each other, like men," the noted myth-teller W.H.D. Rouse pointed out. "They even fought battles like men."[2]

Yet two crucial realities separated the gods from ordinary men and women. First, the gods were far stronger than humans. Second, as Rouse said, the gods "could not kill one another, for they were immortal."[3] Those gods and the humans with whom they mingled populated the Age of Heroes. That was the name the Classical Greeks gave to a legendary era of myth, magic, and adventure in their distant past.

"Classical Greeks" is a modern term. Generally speaking, it denotes the residents of Greece from roughly the 700s to 300s BCE (Before the Common Era). These were the centuries in which the Greeks achieved tremendous progress in the arts, architecture, and literature. Perhaps most notably, they erected the majestic Parthenon in the

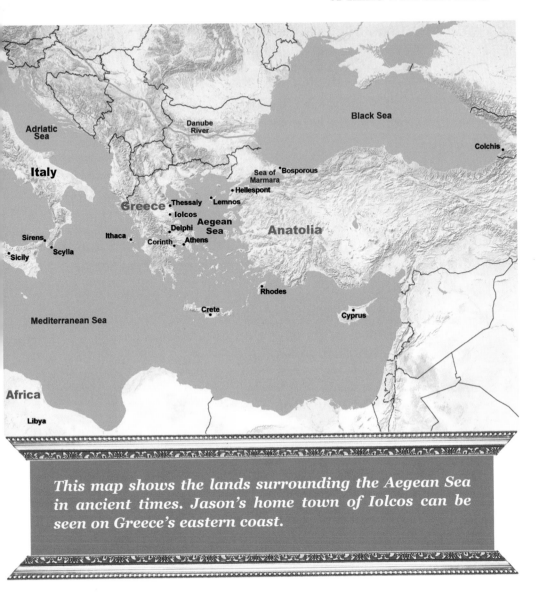

This map shows the lands surrounding the Aegean Sea in ancient times. Jason's home town of Iolcos can be seen on Greece's eastern coast.

city of Athens. The ruins of that imposing religious temple and others like it still grace Greece's striking landscape. The Greeks also invented science, philosophy, democracy, and the theater. For these and other remarkable feats, the Classical Greeks are today viewed as the founders of **Western civilization.**

A Muddled Memory of the Past

Despite their many talents, the Classical Greeks did not have a precise grasp of history. After all, no modern-style history books existed in their era. So they did not know how long before their time the Age of Heroes had actually taken place.

Nor did they realize that this storybook era was largely a muddled memory of an earlier, quite normal Greek society. Modern scholars call that previous period Greece's Bronze Age. It is so named because the main metal used then was **bronze**, a mixture of copper and tin. Late Bronze-Age Greece, which ran from roughly 1600 to 1150 BCE, had two principal power centers. One was on Crete and other islands in the Aegean Sea, which borders the Greek mainland's eastern coast. Greece's other power center in those days consisted of several small kingdoms situated along the mainland's eastern coast.

Sometime in the 1400s BCE, the mainlanders conquered the island-centered realms. They also took over the islanders' trade routes in the Aegean and eastern Mediterranean. The most important city in the northernmost route was Troy, known for its high, sturdy defensive walls. It was located on the western coast of **Anatolia** (what is now Turkey).

Evidence shows that Troy underwent a siege in the late 1200s BCE. And modern historians think the attackers may well have been Greek raiders. If so, this could be the basis for the legendary Trojan War, widely seen as the single most important Greek myth.

The Classical Greeks viewed Jason's quest for the Golden Fleece as very relevant to the Trojan War. This was partly because they used that conflict as a sort of historical milepost. The Greeks believed that Jason and his heroic shipmates lived not long before the Trojan War. If true, Jason, or a real person who inspired his mythical character, was likely born in the late 1300s or early 1200s BCE.

Onset of the Dark Age

Even if such a person did exist, it does not follow that the Golden Fleece and the quest to retrieve it ever existed. The real Jason may have been an early Greek explorer or trader. Perhaps he was the first Greek to establish contact with the faraway land of Colchis. Told and retold over several centuries, the story of this achievement could easily have been exaggerated into an epic adventure.

One reason for the likelihood of such a scenario is that the Bronze Age Greek kingdoms collapsed not long after the Trojan War. The region rapidly sank into a cultural dark age lasting more than three centuries. As the years passed by, reading and writing skills were lost. And the events and leading figures of the remote past—now called the Age of Heroes—became increasingly jumbled, fractured memories.

Eventually, the Greeks recovered from their troubles. They rediscovered writing. And they began to construct a new civilization that would, over time, come to awe and inspire all future ages. An important part of that new culture was the rich collection of myths that had accumulated during the Dark Age. Over time, ancient writers committed these tales to paper. The most vivid version of Jason's story was penned by a Greek named Apollonius (app-uh-LOH-nee-us). He titled his work the *Argonautica*, meaning "Voyage of the Argo."

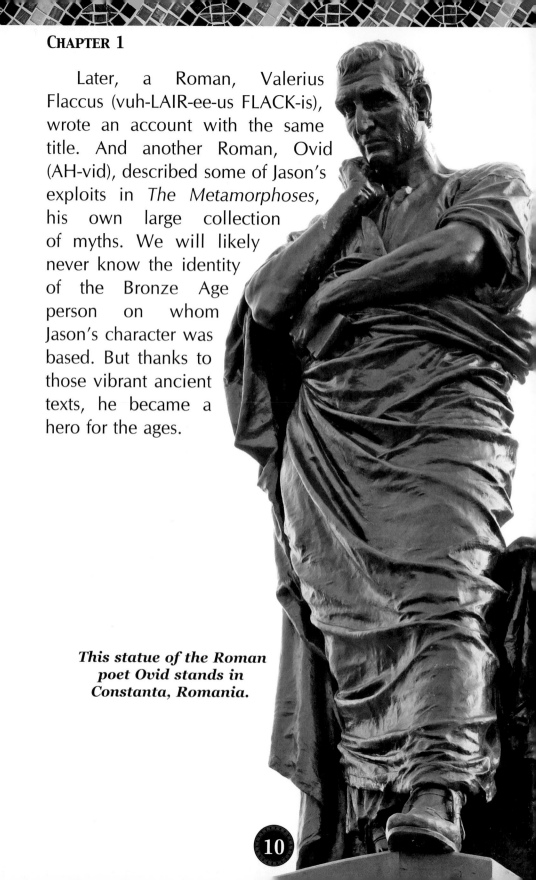

CHAPTER 1

Later, a Roman, Valerius Flaccus (vuh-LAIR-ee-us FLACK-is), wrote an account with the same title. And another Roman, Ovid (AH-vid), described some of Jason's exploits in *The Metamorphoses*, his own large collection of myths. We will likely never know the identity of the Bronze Age person on whom Jason's character was based. But thanks to those vibrant ancient texts, he became a hero for the ages.

This statue of the Roman poet Ovid stands in Constanta, Romania.

JASON THE PIRATE?

Was the real Jason an early Greek explorer who opened up trade with distant Colchis? This is only one of many theories advanced over the years to explain the basis for the Golden Fleece myth.

If true, perhaps Jason brought some exotic rams' hides back to Greece. And over time these hides were exaggerated into a fleece with magical properties.

Another theory suggests that the Fleece was actually a book with pages made from a ram's hide. Supposedly, that volume explained how to turn cheap metals into gold.

Probably the most frequently voiced idea is that the Fleece was a mangled memory of the gold-mining industry that did once exist in Colchis. Evidence shows that miners placed sheep skins in streambeds suspected of containing small particles of gold. After a while, the miners removed the skins, hung them up, and beat them to make the particles fall out. Maybe Jason was a pirate who became widely known for stealing some of these gold-laced fleeces.

A modern artist's conception of the Argo.

The ruins of Apollo's temple at Delphi. Here, a series of oracles supposedly made contact with that god.

THE SINGLE-SANDALED STRANGER

The quest for the Golden Fleece occurred in the generation before the legendary Trojan War. Both of these events occurred during the Age of Heroes, and were linked in some little-known but crucial ways. One link involved a brave young man, Nestor (NES-tuhr), from the Greek city of Pylos. He was one of the heroes Jason selected to join his crew, the celebrated Argonauts. Many years later, Nestor, now an old man, fought in the war at Troy.

Jason, who commanded Nestor and the other Argonauts, was the son of Aeson (EE-sin). And Aeson was himself the son of Cretheus (CREE-thee-uss), the man who had founded Iolcos (ee-OHL-cuss) and became its first king. That thriving city was located on Greece's eastern coast. After Cretheus died, Aeson was in line to take over his father's throne. However, the young man's half-brother, Pelias (puh-LY-us), made sure this did not happen. A dishonest and power-hungry fellow, Pelias schemed to rule Iolcos himself. Backed by soldiers loyal to him, he threw Aeson into prison and seized the throne.

Beware the One-Sandaled Man

Several years went by, during which Aeson married and had children even though he was still in his jail cell. One of these offspring was Jason. Worried that Pelias might try to **slay** the baby, Aeson sent Jason to live with Chiron (KIE-ron) the **centaur**. As the boy grew up, Chiron educated him well. The kind old centaur also revealed that Jason's imprisoned father was Iolcos's true king.

Meanwhile, Pelias worried that some new enemy might appear and threaten his throne. So he consulted the **oracle** at Delphi (DELL-fie), in central Greece. Pelias hoped the gods might give him a preview of what the future held in store for him.

The oracle did not disappoint Iolcos's ruler. Indeed, she told him that serious troubles might lie ahead for him. In particular, he must beware of a stranger wearing just a single sandal. That man, she claimed, might bring about Pelias's downfall.

Now fearful, Pelias returned to Iolcos, where only a few days later the oracle's prediction came true. A strange man wearing only one sandal entered the palace and asked to speak to the king. Standing before Pelias, the visitor introduced himself as his nephew, Jason. On his way to Iolcos, Jason explained, he had lost one of his sandals while crossing a stream. Jason also told Pelias that the time had come for him to step down as king. Aeson should be released and allowed to rule, Jason stated respectfully but firmly.

To Pelias, these were dire words. But he did his best not to show how distressed and angry he was. Thinking on his feet, he politely pretended to agree with Jason. Pelias promised to give up the throne, but on one condition.

This early modern woodcut depicts the friendly, multi-talented centaur Chiron.

Jason must prove he was worthy of ruling the kingdom by performing some difficult feat. Secretly, of course, the king hoped the young man would die while carrying out the exploit. According to Valerius Flaccus's account, Pelias "saw that there were no wars in Greece." Nor were there any monsters roaming the region "that might destroy Jason." Instead, "the dangers of the vast ocean seemed the best way." So Pelias, smiling to mask his deceit, said to Jason, "Go to Colchis, my fine young man. And bring the Golden Fleece back!"[1] If Jason could accomplish this daunting deed, the king declared, the throne would his.

Finding a Worthy Crew

Confident that he could bring back the Fleece, Jason accepted Pelias's challenge. Wasting no time, the young hero immediately set out to find a stout ship. He quickly discovered he had a powerful ally in this effort. She was Athena (uh-THEE-nuh), the goddess of wisdom. At her urging, the well-known shipbuilder Argus traveled to Iolcos. The aging but still vital man pledged that Jason would soon have the finest vessel in all of Greece.

Argus kept that promise. Flaccus described how the magnificent *Argo* rapidly took shape. Trees all around the city "were resounding with the steady blows of the double-edged ax," he wrote. Argus himself sliced "pines with the thin blade of a saw, and the sides of the ship were being

A painting of the Argo by the Italian artist Lorenzo Costa, born in 1460. The vessel looks like the ones in Costa's own era.

fitted together." Meanwhile, bright-eyed Athena hunted for just the right wood "for the sail-carrying mast." Finally "the ship stood finished, strong enough to plow through the pathless sea."[2]

Statue of Athena

A vessel of this quality, Jason realized, must have a crew worthy of her. So he assembled a group of fifty men whose strength and skills were surpassed only by their decency and loyalty. They came to be called the Argonauts, after their ship. Brave Nestor was one. Another was the strongest man in the world—Heracles (HAIR-uh-kleez), whom the Romans later called Hercules (HER-kue-leez).

In his version of the tale, Apollonius mentioned another Argonaut named Hylas (HIE-lus). "A brave comrade in the flower of youth," Hylas went with Heracles "to bear his arrows and to guard his bow."[3] Among the other heroes who sailed with

Jason was a talented musician, Orpheus (OR-fee-us). Calais (kuh-LAY-is) and Zetes (ZEE-teez), the sons of the North Wind, went too, as did broad-shouldered Peleus (puh-LAY-us). Also aboard were Castor (KASS-ter) and Polydeuces (pah-luh-DYOO-seez), the twin sons of Zeus (ZOOS), the chief god. Even old Argus, who had constructed the ship, joined the crew.

An Astounding Sight

When the Argonauts had all boarded the *Argo*, Jason gave the order to cast off. The noble vessel departed Iolcos on its epic voyage. After crossing the Aegean, the Argonauts moved through the Hellespont (now the Dardanelles Strait). That led them into the Propontis (today called the Sea of Marmara).

Soon Jason saw that his crewmen were running low on food and water. So he told them to beach the ship on Bear Mountain, a rugged peninsula that juts out into the Propontis. No sooner had a shore party left to gather provisions when the ship was assaulted. The attackers were hideous, drooling giants, each having six arms.

Fortunately for the Argonauts, brawny Heracles had stayed aboard the ship. In an incredible display of fighting prowess, he killed all the giants. When the other crewmen returned, they were greeted by an astounding sight. Nearly a dozen huge, six-armed bodies were neatly stacked on the beach. After that, the *Argo* set sail once more and headed for the Black Sea's mysterious waters. Jason and the others could only guess at what new dangers might lie ahead.

WAS JASON'S SHIP A PENTEKONTER?

Many modern readers have tried to envision in their mind's eye what Jason's ship, the *Argo*, looked like. No one knows for sure. But most modern scholars think it was a version of a **pentekonter**. That was an early Greek vessel having twenty-five oars on each side. Because the rowers doubled as sailors and fighters, that meant the total number of crewmen was fifty. This agrees with ancient writings that say Jason had about fifty Argonauts.

Researcher Adrian Wood describes the pentekonter in his book about ancient ships. "The rowers sat on benches in the hull," he says. The inside was "not at this time covered by a deck."

There was very little room to store food and water. So the crew had to stop often to gather supplies. The usual way to do this was to beach the ship and scramble ashore. According to Wood, "It was secured by mooring ropes, which could be cut if a rapid departure was required."[4]

A modern model of a Greek pentekonter.

A modern-day bronze statue of Jason's ally, Medea, holds the famous Golden Fleece.

3

FROM COLCHIS TO CRETE

After leaving the Propontis, the *Argo* entered the vast Pontus Axinos. Meaning "unfriendly sea," it is what most Greeks of Jason's day called the Black Sea. They described it that way because its waters were then virtually unknown. A number of Greek vessels had sailed there but never returned. The Argonauts, however, were not "most Greeks." These bold men were unafraid of any obstacles that might stand in the way of their finding the Golden Fleece.

Soon after entering the Black Sea, Jason's vessel skirted the coast of a sparsely populated land later known as Bithynia. While in that area, Heracles' oar broke. So he and his devoted friend Hylas went ashore to look for a tree from which they could cut a new oar.

At some point, the two men were separated, and Heracles was unable to find Hylas. Extremely worried, the strongman searched relentlessly for his friend. In fact, Heracles told Jason he would not leave until he found Hylas. Jason protested, but he soon realized that he had no alternative but to sail on without Heracles and Hylas. Later, a rumor held that Hylas encountered some water **nymphs**—nature spirits who dwelled in a pond. Thinking him handsome, they dragged him into the depths to become their plaything.

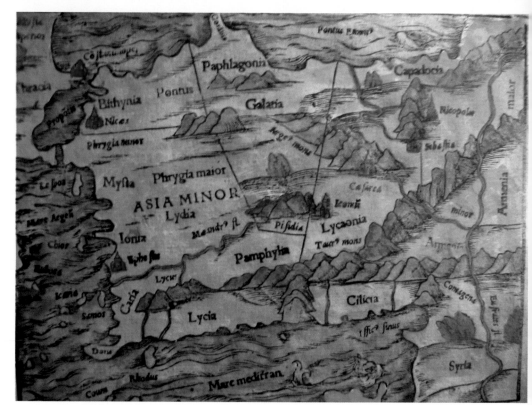

This fifteenth-century map shows Bithynia at the upper left.

The Harpies

The other Argonauts later sorely regretted the loss of mighty Heracles. On several occasions when danger threatened, he would have been a great help. One of those incidents involved the horrifying Harpies (HARP-eez). These flying monsters possessed razor-sharp claws and an awful odor.

The disturbing episode began when the Argonauts beached the ship again to find food. Rounding a bend, they came upon an elderly man who said his name was Phineus (FIN-ee-us). He was so thin and starved-looking that they immediately took pity on him. When Jason asked him to tell his story of woe, Phineus was happy to reply.

Long ago, he told them, the god Apollo had given him the gift of **prophecy**, or foretelling the future. In time, however, Zeus discovered that Phineus had this gift and was enraged that a mere human might have such a powerful skill. So he decided to punish poor Phineus. He blinded him. To make the man's life even more miserable, the hideous Harpies appeared each time the man started eating. "Swooping through the clouds," Apollonius wrote, they "snatched the food away from his mouth and hands. And at times not a morsel of food was left." The creatures also "poured forth over all a **loathsome** stench."[1]

Sons of the North Wind

Appalled, the Argonauts sought to help the pitiful old man. Two of their number—Calais and Zetes—possessed the ability to fly. Their father, after all, was the North Wind. So they became the keys to the plan. First, Jason and the others

A painting on an ancient Italian vase shows a harpy.

collected several bushels of food and placed them before Phineus. As expected, the Harpies suddenly "darted from the clouds,"[2] in Apollonius's words. Just like before, they gulped down the meal and flew away.

But this time, "the two sons of the North Wind flew off in pursuit." Calais and Zetes would surely "have torn them to pieces," with their swords. But the Harpies were saved at the last moment by Iris (I-ris), goddess of the rainbow. It turned out that she was the sister of the disgusting beasts. Please spare the Harpies, she pleaded. And "I myself will give you a pledge that hereafter they shall not draw near to Phineus."[3] Iris kept her word. Phineus was finally able to eat his meals in peace.

Happy to have helped the old man, the Argonauts sailed on to Colchis. Going ashore, Jason introduced himself to the ruler of that land, Aeetes (ay-EE-teez). At first, the king was friendly and invited the chief Argonaut to dinner. But then Jason got right to the point and requested that Aeetes hand over the Golden Fleece. At this, the king's mood markedly changed. "His heart was filled high in **wrath**," as Apollonius told it. Thinking that the Greeks had come to steal his throne, Aeetes shouted "Begone from my sight!"[4]

A Secret Weapon

Jason insisted that he had come only for the Fleece. But even if that was true, Aeetes said, Jason was wasting his time. According to local custom, no one could take the Fleece unless he first proved his courage. And the test of that valor seemed to be far too difficult for any person to accomplish. It consisted of several parts, each one of which was very risky and dangerous.

First, Jason would have to tame two huge, fire-breathing bulls. Then he must harness them and use them to plow the teeth of a dragon into the soil. Those teeth, Aeetes added, would almost instantly grow into a hundred fearsome warriors. And the plowman would have to defeat them all.

In the unlikely event that the plowman was successful, the king pointed out, the Fleece was guarded by a terrifying serpent that never slept. Anyone who tried to take the golden hide would have to deal with that bloodthirsty beast.

Such feats did sound almost impossible to Jason, and he nearly gave up the quest. But then, seemingly out of nowhere, he received some unexpected aid. Aeetes' beautiful daughter, Medea (meh-DEE-uh), had fallen in love with Jason at first sight. Who could "fail to be stirred by his youth, his noble birth, his valor?"[5] she asked herself in Ovid's version of the myth.

Medea was so taken with Jason that she decided to help him. As it happened, she had considerable knowledge of magic. So she gave him some magical oil. When rubbed onto the skin, she told him, it made a person immensely strong. This secret weapon did the trick for Jason. He became so powerful that he easily tamed the bulls. He also defeated the warriors who grew from the dragon's teeth.

Then Jason approached the fierce serpent that guarded the Fleece. "It was a striking sight, this creature," Ovid wrote. It had a jagged crest on its head and a "three-forked tongue and curving fangs."[6] Yet though it was indeed both frightening and fearsome, it was no match for Jason's larger-than-normal strength. He swiftly slew the monster and grabbed the Fleece. In some versions of the story,

Jason confronts the serpent in this
painting on a dinner plate made
in England in the 1500s.

Jason didn't fight the dragon. Instead, Medea gave it a magic potion that put it to sleep. Either way, Jason and Medea boarded the *Argo*, which hastily set sail for Greece.

Pleased with himself, Jason was certain that his troubles would soon be over. The rightful king would be back on Iolcos's throne. At that moment, the Fleece's new caretaker had no inkling of how dead wrong he was.

MEMORIES OF THERA'S VOLCANO?

During the four months it took the Argonauts to return home, they encountered several more dangers. One took place near the island of Crete and involved a bronze giant named Talos. At Zeus's order, he patrolled the island and kept strangers away by hurling enormous boulders at them. The *Argo* suffered a rain of these lethal missiles. The ship might have been destroyed if Medea had not employed her magic to defeat the powerful Talos.

Some modern scholars suggest that this part of Jason's myth may be based on dim memories of a real event. Just north of Crete lies the small island of Thera (also known as Santorini). In the late Bronze Age, probably about 1650 BCE, a massive volcano on Thera violently erupted. Among other things, it blew huge rocks outward over long distances. Any sailors who had near-misses with those volcanic bombs would have told everyone they knew about their narrow escape. It certainly is possible that exaggerated versions of such stories later became part of the myth of the Argonauts' voyage.

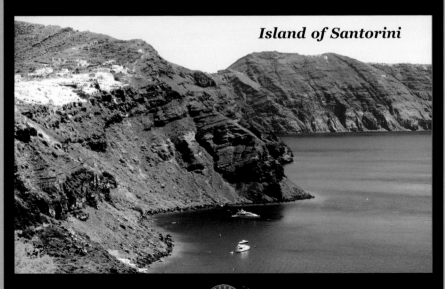

Island of Santorini

This painting of Jason and the Fleece is by Belgian artist Erasmus Quellinus (1607–1678).

4

JASON AND MEDEA IN CORINTH

When the *Argo* finally returned to Iolcos, Jason disbanded the fellowship of the Argonauts. Each hero went his separate way and later experienced new adventures of his own. In addition, some of the Argonauts' sons became renowned heroes in their own right. Broad-shouldered Peleus, for example, fathered Achilles (uh-KILL-eez), the greatest warrior of the Trojan War.

As for Jason, he proudly carried the Golden Fleece to Iolcos's palace and presented it to King Pelias. But that shifty ruler went back on his prior promise. He flatly refused to **abdicate**, or step down from his throne, as he had earlier claimed he would.

Jason was naturally angry at being cheated this way. He stubbornly continued his dispute with Pelias, hoping to get his father, Aeson, released. The months rolled by and soon became years. During that time, Jason and Medea took up temporary residence in Iolcos. As husband and wife, they were graced with several children.

Medea Helps Out Again
Because she loved Jason so much, Medea also came to hate Pelias for his dishonesty. So she finally decided

to do something to obtain justice. As it turned out, that something was quite drastic. Medea met in secret with Pelias's three daughters and convinced them to cut their father up into little pieces. Medea said she would sprinkle some magic herbs onto those fragments. Pelias would then be reborn as a strong, handsome young man.

"Draw your swords," Medea urged the princesses. "Drain out the old blood" from your father's body. Then "I can fill his emptied veins with that of youth."[1] The young women agreed to this horrible scheme and butchered their father. But to their shock and grief, no resurrection occurred. Just as Medea had planned, Pelias was dead. Permanently dead.

Medea had managed to help Jason achieve revenge on Pelias. Yet the king's grisly murder only made things worse for the man who had captured the famous Fleece. The new king, Pelias's son Acastus (uh-CASS-tis) was enraged. He drove Jason, Medea, and their children out of Iolcos. Desperate, the family traveled southward and settled in the city of Corinth.

Not long after this move, Jason did something that surprised everyone who knew him. He suddenly abandoned his wife for another woman. She was Glauce (GLOH-see), daughter of Corinth's king, Creon (KREE-on). Some people suggested that Jason did it for power. On Creon's death, Glauce would become Corinth's queen, and that would make Jason the city's king.

Whatever Jason's reasons for being unfaithful, Medea was crushed. Some of the townspeople "heard her sobbing and wailing," wrote the Greek playwright Euripides (yer-IPP-uh-deez). Over and over, Medea shouted harsh words "against her husband who had betrayed her." Among these words were "May I see Jason and his bride ground to pieces in their shattered palace!"[2]

Indeed, Medea was so upset and said so many hurtful things that many people became concerned. In particular, the king worried that she might seek revenge on Jason and Glauce. So Creon banished Medea and her children from the city. At that point, she suddenly changed her tone. In a calmer voice, Medea begged the king to at least give her one full day to prepare for her exile. Thinking it only fair, he granted that request.

A "Filthy Coward?"

Medea's more peaceful manner was only an act, however. Inside, she was still seething with anger. During the day she had been given, she fully expected to achieve her revenge. Not realizing the true depth of her rage, Jason tried to reason with her. He said that her "ungoverned rage" was the cause of her troubles, not his actions. "You could have stayed in Corinth," he told her, "and still lived in this house." Instead, he continued, "you talked like a fool. And now you're banished." Even so, "I will not desert a friend,"[3] he added. He offered her some money to make her upcoming move easier.

Medea scorned the offer. She screamed "You filthy coward! You have the wickedness to turn me out, to get yourself another wife, even after I had borne you sons!" To this, Jason could only say, "I have done my best to help you." But "you make no response to kindness." Therefore, "so much the worst for you!"[4] Then he stormed out.

Some servants heard this heated exchange. Within hours the entire city knew all about the harsh words that the two had exchanged with each other. Many citizens now felt that the once widely respected Jason had become a fallen hero. At the same time, they pitied Medea in her current plight.

But this sympathy for her did not last long. To everyone's utter horror, a few hours later Medea exacted her horrific revenge. Pretending to apologize for her crude words, she sent young Glauce a splendid new gown. The delighted princess wasted no time in trying it on. Too late, she discovered that the garment was laced with acid, which burned her skin off. Mere seconds later, she was dead. Seeing his daughter collapse in agony, King Creon ran to her side. Unwisely, he embraced her, and the acid killed him too.

Even worse, Medea slew two of her own children. Her desire to see Jason suffer had plainly surpassed her love for those boys. She knew that losing his sons would tear him apart. And it did. In tears, he asked her, "You could endure—a mother!—to lift sword against your own little ones? May the gods blast your life!"[5]

Whether or not the gods did in fact punish Medea for child-murder remains uncertain. It is rumored that after her exile from Corinth, she lived in Athens for a while. Eventually she returned to Colchis. What is certain is that several gods did abandon Jason for his cruel treatment of Medea. Among them was Zeus's wife, Hera (HEAR-uh).

Thereafter, Jason led a lonely, gloomy life. One day when he was middle-aged, he came upon his old ship, the *Argo*, rotting away on a beach. He fell asleep beneath the vessel's stern, or back end. It suddenly collapsed, killing him. Few people were surprised when they heard the news. For this was the sort of commonplace, embarrassing end the gods often handed out to fallen heroes.

DRAMATIZING THE GREEK MYTHS

Euripides, who wrote about Jason's and Medea's troubles in Corinth in his play *Medea*, was one of Greece's greatest playwrights. He was born in Athens in the early 400s BCE.

Writers and artists in Athens had invented the theater a few decades earlier. Euripides and his fellow playwrights constantly experimented with new theatrical forms and ideas. These later became the standards for dramatic works for the Western world right up to the present time.

Altogether, Euripides composed eighty-eight plays. But of these, just nineteen have survived. Like *Medea* (written in 431 BCE), they mostly dramatize famous Greek myths. Also, as shown by Jason and Medea in that play, Euripides was highly skilled at creating very realistic, believable characters. Indeed, his works, which are still performed around the world, often sound like they were recently written.

Actress Elizabeth Pozzi plays Medea in a modern production of Euripides' play.

A statue of the great Greek playwright Euripides holds a
mask of tragedy, his area of expertise.

JASON'S MYTHS IN POP CULTURE

Euripides, Apollonius, Ovid, and other Greek and Roman writers composed the first written accounts of Jason's myths. Ever since, writers have been inspired by them. So have painters, sculptors, and other artists of all kinds. Each produced his or her own version of the search for the Fleece and Jason's betrayal of Medea. As a result, these mythical tales have become regular features of popular culture. Often called "**pop culture**" for short, it includes familiar themes, ideas, sayings, and images that most Americans, British, and other Westerners share.

After **Greco-Roman** society fell apart in the 400s and 500s CE (Common Era) many people still recalled the old myths. They told and retold them **orally**, which means by word of mouth. Slowly but steadily, Western writers and artists created works based on one or more of those stories.

One of the earliest pop culture versions of Jason's quest for the Golden Fleece appeared in the 1500s in England. Edmund Spenser penned the long poetic fantasy *The Faerie Queene*. Among many other references to the Greek myths, it cites Jason's "goodly conquest of the Golden Fleece," and "the wondrous Argo."[1] Spenser's

countryman, playwright William Shakespeare, also mentioned Jason and the Fleece in *The Merchant of Venice* (1596).

Famous playwright William Shakespeare, along with the title page of his play The Merchant of Venice.

Music and Painting

In the decades that followed, musical composers found fertile fields of ideas in the old Greco-Roman myths. Opera—consisting of stage plays in which all or most of the lines are sung—was rapidly becoming popular. Jason's quest was just the kind of larger-than-life story that worked well in that new musical medium. In 1649, therefore, Italian composer Pier Francesco Cavalli created the opera *Giasone* (the Italian spelling of Jason). Extremely popular, it has been performed often over the years. Among the most recent productions were in Chicago in 2010 and London in 2013.

Characters and incidents from Jason's myths have also been captured in paintings. Indeed, hundreds of them have appeared over the centuries. One of the most beautiful is by Biagio d'Antonio, an Italian artist of the late 1400s. His work, *Scenes from the Story of the Argonauts* (ca. 1465), shows half a dozen episodes from the myth on one canvas. Much more recent is noted English artist John William Waterhouse's *Jason and Medea*. Painted in 1907, it depicts the couple in Colchis shortly before Jason tames the bulls.

There have been numerous **literary** versions of Jason's story as well. Particularly well-known were books written for children during a surge of interest in the Greek myths in the 1800s. In 1853, American author Nathaniel Hawthorne produced *Tanglewood Tales*, a collection of such stories that includes Jason. Three years later, the equally admired English storyteller Charles Kingsley tackled the quest for the Fleece in *The Heroes*. Instant hits, both volumes were

Biagio d'Antonio's splendid Scenes from the Story of the Argonauts *now rests in New York City's Metropolitan Museum of Art.*

frequently reissued in the twentieth century and many people still read them today.

Heroes Reborn in Flesh and Blood

One drawback to Hawthorne's and Kingsley's works is that their tellings of Jason's myth are fairly short. A much longer version appeared in 1867. The author was English poet and craftsman William Morris. His *The Life and Death of Jason* is some 7,500 lines long. Morris's rather flowery writing style is evident in his description of the frightening Harpies:

> Behold the daughters of the earth and sea,
> The dreadful snatchers, who like women were
> Down to the breast, with scanty coarse
>   black hair
> About their heads and dim eyes ringed with red,
> And bestial mouths set round with lips of lead,
> But for their gnarled [twisted] necks there began
>   to spring
> Half-hair, half-feathers, and a sweeping wing.[2]

The many poems, books, paintings, and musical pieces about Jason are clearly vivid and engaging. Yet each is known only to a fairly small number of people. Far larger are the audiences for plays and movies about Jason, Medea, and the quest for the Fleece.

Euripides' play *Medea*, for instance, is still performed often in Europe, America, and elsewhere. In the past century, the actress most famous for playing the title character was England's Judith Anderson. She won a Tony Award for playing Medea in 1947. The great English actor

The late, great Judith Anderson as she appeared onstage in Euripides' Medea in the 1940s.

John Gielgud played Jason in that production. Anderson revived the role in 1951, 1955, and still again in 1959 in a TV version.

According to some film historians, movies and the Greek myths were made for each other. Motion pictures, they say, made it possible for the first time ever to reenact the Greek myths in a realistic manner. And on the big screen, heroes like Jason and his shipmates are in a sense reborn in flesh and blood.

So even more people are familiar with Jason's myths thanks to the movie *Jason and the Argonauts*, which was released in 1963. It does take some liberties here and there with Apollonius's original telling. Yet it is still hugely entertaining. First, it portrays Zeus, Hermes, and the other gods just as the Classical Greeks envisioned them—as huge, powerful beings. In contrast, Jason is portrayed as the size of a chess piece on a game-board in Zeus's palace atop Mt. Olympus.

The film is also exceptional for its special effects, which bring the Harpies and other mythical creatures to life. Behind this visual magic was the great early modern effects wizard Ray Harryhausen. Today's **digital effects** (sometimes called computer-generated imagery, or CGI) had not yet been invented. Instead, he animated movable puppets, photographing them one **film frame** at a time. His mastery of this process made the bronze giant Talos and the serpent that guarded the Fleece seem incredibly real. In fact, one expert says, these effects, and the film overall, keep Jason's ancient tale fresh in the public imagination. They bring "mythological creatures and the gods of ancient Greece to life in a way never before seen, and never since surpassed."[3]

A New Dimension of Reality

Ray Harryhausen (1920–2013) did not invent the stop-motion animation process. But he brought it to its height of on-screen realism.

That process begins with a small model, or puppet, of the animal or object one wants to come alive in a film. The model has many flexible joints. These allow animators to move its head, arms, or other parts into any position. They make small adjustments and then snap a single frame of film. The procedure is repeated over and over again.

Later, the thousands of film frames created this way run through a projector at normal speed (24 frames per second). And the model appears to move, even though it was always perfectly still when the animator photographed it. Harryhausen spent close to two years animating the mythical monsters for *Jason and the Argonauts*. And that effort still marks the **zenith**, or high point, of artistic recreations of the Greek myths. Film historian Jon Solomon wrote of "Harryhausen's genius," which took "the Greek mythological world into a new dimension of visual reality."[4]

Ray Harryhausen poses with his model of the monster Medusa, which he animated for the 1981 film Clash of the Titans.

CHAPTER NOTES

Chapter 1: A Hero for the Ages
1. Philip Wilkinson, *The Illustrated Dictionary of Mythology* (New York: Dorling Kindersley, 2006), p. 12.
2. W.H.D. Rouse, *Gods, Heroes and Men of Ancient Greece* (New York: New American Library, 2001), p. x.
3. Ibid.

Chapter 2: The Single-Sandaled Stranger
1. Rhoda A. Hendricks, editor and translator, *Classical Gods and Heroes: Myths as Told by the Ancient Authors* (New York: Morrow Quill, 1974), p. 182.
2. Ibid., p. 183.
3. Apollonius, *The Argonautica*, translated by R.C. Seaton (New York: Global Grey, 2014), p. 4.
4. Adrian K. Wood, *Warships of the Ancient World, 3000-500 B.C.* (New York: Osprey, 2012), pp. 32, 35.

Chapter 3: From Colchis to Crete
1. Apollonius, *The Argonautica*, translated by R.C. Seaton (New York: Global Grey, 2014), p. 115.
2. Ibid., p. 121.
3. Ibid., pp. 121, 123.
4. Ibid., p. 219.
5. Ovid, *Metamorphoses*, translated by Mary M. Innes (London: Penguin, 1955), p. 156.
6. Ibid., p. 159.

Chapter 4: Jason and Medea in Corinth
1. Ovid, *Metamorphoses*, translated by Mary M. Innes (London: Penguin, 1955), p. 164.
2. Euripides, *Medea*, translated by Philip Vellacott (New York: Penguin, 1984), pp. 22–23.
3. Ibid., pp. 30-31.
4. Ibid., pp. 31, 35.
5. Ibid., p. 58.

Chapter 5: Jason's Myths in Pop Culture
1. Edmund Spenser, *The Faerie Queene*, Book 2, Canto 12. Bartleby.com. http://www.bartleby.com/331/409.html

CHAPTER NOTES

2. William Morris, *The Life and Death of Jason* (Boston: Roberts Brothers, 1867), p. 85.

3. Ruth Merriam, "Of Men and Gods, and the Monsters Thereof: A Review of *Jason and the Argonauts*." Monster Awareness Month. http://monsterawarenessmonth.wordpress.com/2011/02/12/of -men-and-gods-and-the-monsters-thereof-a-review-of-jason-and -the-argonauts/

4. Jon Solomon, *The Ancient World in the Cinema* (New Haven: Yale University Press, 2001), p. 115.

WORKS CONSULTED

Apollonius of Rhodes. *Argonautica*. Translated by Aaron Poochigian. New York: Penguin, 2014.

Bellingham, David. *An Introduction to Greek Mythology*. Secaucus, NJ: Chartwell Books, 1989.

Bowra, C.M. *Classical Greece*. New York: Time-Life, 1977.

Burkert, Walter. *Greek Religion, Archaic and Classical*. Oxford, England: Basil Blackwell, 1985.

Butler, James H. *The Theater and Drama of Greece and Rome*. San Francisco, CA: Chandler Publishing, 1972.

Colavito, Jason. *Jason and the Argonauts Through the Ages*. Jefferson, NC: McFarland, 2014.

Drews, Robert. *The End of the Bronze Age: Changes in Warfare and the Catastrophe ca. 1200 B.C.* Princeton, NJ: Princeton University Press, 1995.

Euripides. *Medea*. Translated by Philip Vellacott. New York: Penguin, 1984.

Fitten, J. Lesley. *Discovery of the Greek Bronze Age*. London: British Museum Press, 1995.

Grant, Michael. *A Guide to the Ancient World*. New York: Barnes and Noble, 1997.

Grant, Michael. *The Myths of the Greeks and Romans*. New York: Plume, 1995.

Grant, Michael and John Hazel. *Who's Who in Classical Mythology*. London: Routledge, 2002.

Hamilton, Edith. *Mythology*. New York: Grand Central, 1999.

Harryhausen, Ray. *Ray Harryhausen: An Animated Life*. New York: Billboard, 2004.

Works Consulted

Hendricks, Rhoda A., editor and translator. *Classical Gods and Heroes: Myths as Told by the Ancient Authors*. New York: Morrow Quill, 1974.

Howatson, M.C. and Ian Chilvers, editors. *The Concise Oxford Companion to Classical Literature*. New York: Oxford University Press, 2007.

Levi, Peter. *The Penguin History of Greek Literature*. New York: Penguin, 1987.

Martin, Thomas R. *Ancient Greece: From Prehistoric to Hellenistic Times*. New Haven: Yale University Press, 2000.

Matyszak, Philip. *The Greek and Roman Myths: A Guide to the Classical Stories*. London: Thames and Hudson, 2010.

Morford, Mark P.O. and Robert J. Lenardon, *Classical Mythology*. New York: Oxford University Press, 2010.

Rouse, W.H.D. *Gods, Heroes and Men of Ancient Greece*. New York: New American Library, 2001.

Solomon, Jon. *The Ancient World in the Cinema*. New Haven, CT: Yale University Press, 2001.

Stapleton, Michael. *The Illustrated Dictionary of Greek and Roman Mythology*. New York: Peter Bedrick, 1986.

Webster, T.B.L. *From Mycenae to Homer*. New York: Routledge, 2014.

Wood, Adrian K. *Warships of the Ancient World, 3000-500 B.C.* New York: Osprey, 2012.

Further Reading

Baumann, Susan K. *Jason and the Golden Fleece*. New York: Power Kids Press, 2014.

Colum, Padraic. *The Golden Fleece and the Heroes Who Lived Before Achilles*. San Diego, CA: Didactic Press, 2013.

Daly, Kathleen N. *Greek and Roman Mythology A to Z*. New York: Chelsea House, 2009.

Green, Roger L. *Tales of the Greek Heroes*. London: Puffin, 2009.

Kingsley, Charles. *The Heroes*. Santa Barbara, CA: Mission Audio, 2011.

Lovatt, Helen. *In Search of the Argonauts: The Remarkable History of Jason and the Golden Fleece*. London: I.B. Tauris, 2015.

ON THE INTERNET

Adams, David. "Georgia: In Search of Jason and the Argonauts."
http://www.davidadamsfilms.com.au/projects/journeys/georgia-in-search-of-jason-and-the-argonauts/

"The Argonauts." Greek Mythology Link.
http://www.maicar.com/GML/ARGONAUTS.html

Harrod, Horatia. "Ray Harryhausen: master of animation." *The Telegraph*, May 8, 2010.
http://www.telegraph.co.uk/culture/film/film-life/7593495/Ray-Harryhausen-interview-Stop-motion-animation-Clash-of-the-Titans-Jason-and-the-Argonauts.html

"Hercules." Theoi Greek Mythology.
http://www.theoi.com/greek-mythology/heracles.html

"In Search of Ancient Heroes: Jason and the Argonauts." PBS.
http://www.pbs.org/mythsandheroes/myths_four_jason.html

"Jason." Encyclopedia Mythica.
http://www.pantheon.org/articles/j/jason.html

"Jason." Greek Mythology Link.
http://www.maicar.com/GML/Jason.html

"Jason." Mythweb.
http://www.mythweb.com/heroes/Jason/

"Jason and the Argonauts: Special Effects." YouTube.
http://www.youtube.com/watch?v=w-1z7n3yoKs

"Medea." Encylopedia Mythica.
http://www.pantheon.org/articles/m/medea.html

Merriam, Ruth. "Of Men and Gods, and the Monsters Thereof: *A Review of Jason and the Argonauts*."
http://monsterawarenessmonth.wordpress.com/2011/02/12/of-men-and-gods-and-the-monsters-thereof-a-review-of-jason-and-the-argonauts/

"Talos." Theoi Greek Mythology.
http://www.theoi.com/Gigante/GiganteTalos.html

GLOSSARY

abdicate (AB-duh-kate)—to step down from or give up a throne or other position of power

Anatolia (an-uh-TOLL-ya)—also called Asia Minor; the land mass today comprising modern-day Turkey; in ancient times, its western sector along the Aegean Sea was a Greek cultural area

bronze (BRONZ)—a mixture of copper and tin

centaur (SEN-tohr)—in Greek mythology, a being that is half-human and half-horse

digital effects (DIJ-uh-tuhl eh-FEKTS) or CGI (see-gee-EYE)—movie special effects method in which two groups of people or objects are filmed separately and those pieces of film are scanned into a computer, where the elements are combined to appear that both groups of people or objects look like they were photographed in the same place at the same time

film frame (FILM fraim)—a tiny single photo taken by a movie camera; when the film runs through a projector, the fast-moving still photos create the illusion of movement

Greco-Roman (GREK-oh-ROH-muhn)—having to do with the merger of ancient Greek and Roman cultures during and after Rome's conquest of the Greek kingdoms and city-states in the 200s and 100s BCE

literary (LIT-uh-rair-ee)—having to do with literature

loathsome (LOHTH-sum)—disgusting

nymphs (NIMFS)—in Greek mythology, minor goddesses or nature spirits

oracle (OR-uh-kuhl)—in the ancient world, a priestess who supposedly relayed messages from a god to humans; also the place she did this and the message itself

orally (OR-uh-lee)—by word of mouth

pentekonter (PEN-tuh-KON-ter)—an early Greek ship having twenty-five oars on each side

pop culture (POP KUL-cher)—short for "popular" culture, it includes familiar themes, ideas, sayings, and images that most Americans, British, and other Westerners share

prophecy (PRAH-fuh-see)—a prediction about future events

slay (SLAY)—to kill

stop-motion animation (STOP-moh-shin an-uh-MAY-shun)—the film process in which a model or puppet is photographed one frame at a time and later run through a projector to create the illusion that the model is moving

Western civilization (WEST-ern siv-uh-li-ZAY-shun)—the culture or society that developed over time in Europe and the places colonized by Europeans around the world, including the United States, Australia, and New Zealand

wrath (RATH)—anger

zenith (ZEE-nith)—the highest height of something

INDEX

ABOUT THE AUTHOR

Historian and award-winning writer Don Nardo has published more than four hundred books for teens and children, along with a number of volumes for college and general adult readers. His specialty is the ancient world, including the histories, cultures, and myths of the Egyptians, Greeks, Romans, and peoples of Mesopotamia. Mr. Nardo, who also composes and arranges orchestral music, lives with his wife Christine in Massachusetts.